96 FACTS ABOUT BEYONCÉ

Quizzes, QUOTES, QUESTIONS, and MORE!

BY ARIE KAPLAN
ILLUSTRATED BY Risa Rodil

Grosset & Dunlap

GROSSET & DUNLAP
An imprint of Penguin Random House LLC
1745 Broadway, New York, New York 10019

First published in the United States of America by Grosset & Dunlap,
an imprint of Penguin Random House LLC, 2025

Text copyright © 2025 by Arie Kaplan, LLC
Illustrations copyright © 2025 by Risa Rodil

Photo credits: (geometric bee) Karno Muji Saputra/iStock/Getty Images,
(honeycomb) Farhan T. Sudibya/iStock/Getty Images

Penguin Random House values and supports copyright. Copyright fuels creativity, encourages diverse voices, promotes free speech, and creates a vibrant culture. Thank you for buying an authorized edition of this book and for complying with copyright laws by not reproducing, scanning, or distributing any part of it in any form without permission. You are supporting writers and allowing Penguin Random House to continue to publish books for every reader. Please note that no part of this book may be used or reproduced in any manner for the purpose of training artificial intelligence technologies or systems.

GROSSET & DUNLAP is a registered trademark of
Penguin Random House LLC.

Visit us online at penguinrandomhouse.com.

Manufactured in Canada

ISBN 9780593891506   10 9 8 7 6 5 4 3 2 1 FRI

Design by Kimberley Sampson

The publisher does not have any control over and does not assume any responsibility for author or third-party websites or their content.

The authorized representative in the EU for product safety and compliance is Penguin Random House Ireland, Morrison Chambers, 32 Nassau Street, Dublin D02 YH68, Ireland, https://eu-contact.penguin.ie.

TABLE OF CONTENTS

Part I
Bey's Beginnings 4

Part II
Embracing Her Destiny 20

Part III
Going Solo 36

Part IV
Different Themes, Different Genres 52

Part V
Filmmaking and Future Endeavors 68

BEY'S BEGINNINGS
All Hail the Queen

    Often nicknamed "Queen Bey," Beyoncé Knowles-Carter is a trailblazing singer, songwriter, dancer, actor, filmmaker, and businesswoman. Some consider her the world's greatest living entertainer, which is unsurprising given her many talents. Beyoncé's influence on the culture at large is monumental. Every album she drops, every video she releases, every brand she endorses, every social media post she likes—when Beyoncé does something, it gets people talking.

    But who *is* Beyoncé, really? Who is she as a person? What challenges has she overcome? How did she become the star she is today?

    Read on to find out the answers to those questions, and many more!

BEY BITS!

Beyoncé is so famous, she's often known simply by her first name, just like fellow "single name" pop stars Madonna, Cher, Britney, and Adele! You might even call them "all the single-*name* ladies"!

As of February 2024, Beyoncé was the most nominated female artist in the history of the Grammy Awards, with eighty-eight career nominations and thirty-two wins.

Shy but Strong

Beyoncé Giselle Knowles was born in Houston, Texas, on September 4, 1981. When she was a child, Beyoncé was shy and introverted. And even though there's nothing wrong with being shy, Beyoncé's parents, Mathew and Tina, were concerned that she was becoming too fearful to truly enjoy her childhood. In order to bolster Beyoncé's confidence, her mother signed her up for dance lessons when she was seven years old.

Beyoncé enjoyed the lessons, and she practiced very hard. Her dance teacher, Darlette Johnson, noticed that Beyoncé was not only a good dancer; she also had an incredible singing voice. Darlette told Beyoncé's parents that their daughter should sing in a local talent show. Would Beyoncé do it? Would this shy, quiet girl get up onstage and sing in front of an audience?

Beyoncé's first name is a tribute to her mother Tina's maiden name, which is *also* Beyoncé.

On June 24, 1986, Beyoncé's sister, Solange, was born.

Trophies and Triumphs

Beyoncé's parents thought she should enter the talent show. So she did. Right before the show started, she was very nervous. But as soon as Beyoncé began singing, she commanded the mic, instantly winning over the audience! Even though she was only seven years old and most of the other contestants were teenagers, Beyoncé won the talent show!

After that, she entered many more talent shows and singing contests—during the next few years, she competed in over fifty of them. Beyoncé's bedroom was soon bursting with trophies from all the competitions she won!

The song Beyoncé sang at that first talent show was the classic John Lennon tune "Imagine."

Beyoncé's mother, Tina, created stylish, colorful outfits for each contest she participated in.

Girl's Tyme

In 1990, nine-year-old Beyoncé auditioned for—and won—a spot in a girl group that was being assembled in Houston. The group was called Girl's Tyme, and its membership fluctuated for a while. Throughout the first year, there were thirty girls circulating in and out of the group. Eventually this was pared down to five: Beyoncé, LaTavia Roberson, Ashley Támar Davis, and sisters Nina and Nikki Taylor. The sixth lasting member to be brought on was Kelendria "Kelly" Rowland. Beyoncé was one of the lead singers, and the girls rehearsed for up to eight hours a day.

A few years later, Girl's Tyme was on a television show called *Star Search*, where they competed against another musical act . . . and lost. But why? Perhaps there were too many people in the group. Eventually, Ashley, Nina, and Nikki left Girl's Tyme, and a girl named LeToya Luckett joined the group.

Now Girl's Tyme had *four* members. Would this smaller version of the group be a success?

In the 1980s and 1990s, *Star Search* was one of the most popular talent competitions on American television.

Beyoncé and Kelly got along really well, since they were both shy, sensitive girls.

Fierce Facts

1 When Beyoncé was around a year old—before she could even walk—she tried to dance!

2 When Beyoncé was growing up, her father, Mathew, was a sales executive for the Xerox corporation.

3 Around the same time, Beyoncé's mother, Tina, ran a hair salon called Headliners.

4 Tina's full given name, including her surname, is Célestine Ann Beyoncé.

5 When Tina was a teenager, she was in a singing group called the Veltones.

6 Beyoncé and her sister Solange were very close while growing up.

7 Andretta Tillman was the initial manager of Girl's Tyme in 1990 and got them gigs performing at small venues in Texas.

8 After Girl's Tyme's performance on *Star Search*, Mathew Knowles began comanaging the group alongside Andretta.

9 Kelly Rowland had a tough childhood; her father was out of the picture, and her mother was working hard to make ends meet.

10 Because of this, the Knowles family took Kelly in and let her live with them.

From Fearful to Fearless

"I remember walking out and I was scared, but when the music started, I don't know what happened. I just... changed."

—Beyoncé on performing in that first talent show

Have you ever been afraid to do something, but when you actually did it, the fear went away? What was that like? Write about it on the lines below.

_____
_____
_____
_____
_____
_____
_____
_____
_____
_____
_____
_____
_____
_____
_____
_____
_____
_____
_____
_____

After-School Activities

Shortly after Beyoncé's first talent show performance, she joined the children's choir at St. John's United Methodist Church. She really enjoyed it! Do you participate in after-school or extracurricular activities? If so, which ones do you like the most? Write about it on the lines below.

Queen Bey Quiz: Growing Up

1) The hospital where Beyoncé was born was called ____.

   a. The X-Mansion
   b. The Fortress of Solitude
   c. The Batcave
   d. Park Plaza Hospital

2) Even though Beyoncé was shy, when she was five years old, she would ____ for family members in the living room of her house.

   a. Fly
   b. Sing
   c. Teleport
   d. Shape-shift

3) When Beyoncé was young, one of her musical heroes was ____.

   a. George Washington
   b. Abraham Lincoln
   c. Prince
   d. Theodore Roosevelt

4) Beyoncé's father, Mathew, is from ____.
    a. Gadsden, Alabama
    b. Disneyland
    c. Disney World
    d. Disneyland Paris

5) Beyoncé's mother, Tina, is from ____.
    a. Narnia
    b. Middle Earth
    c. The Matrix
    d. Galveston, Texas

Check your answers on page 78!

EMBRACING HER DESTINY

A New Name

After their appearance on *Star Search*, Girl's Tyme spent much of their time performing at small gatherings and events in Houston. Beyoncé's dad, Mathew, thought that the group needed a new name to project a more mature image. From then on, they were known as Destiny's Child.

In 1996, the group auditioned for executives at Columbia Records. Beyoncé and her friends tried their hardest ... and it worked. They got a record deal! Destiny's Child was about to hit the big time.

According to Beyoncé's mom, Tina, the name "Destiny's Child" came about because she saw the word *destiny* in the Bible.

And then Beyoncé's dad, Mathew, added the word *child* to *destiny*, giving the group formerly known as Girl's Tyme a truly memorable new name.

The Debut Drops

By early 1997, Destiny's Child had finished recording the vast majority of their first album. But they'd have to wait the better part of a year before it came out. In the meantime, however, they gave fans a taste of what to expect. In October 1997, Destiny's Child's debut single, "No, No, No," dropped. It eventually soared to number three on the *Billboard* Hot 100.

Other singles were released throughout the next few months, until at last, the group's self-titled debut album, *Destiny's Child*, hit stores on February 17, 1998. The album did okay, but it wasn't a smash. It was a ballad-heavy, traditional R&B album, and in the years since it came out, Beyoncé has said that the songs on *Destiny's Child* sounded too mature and serious for a group that consisted of teenagers.

"R&B" stands for "Rhythm and Blues."

R&B is a musical genre influenced by gospel, jazz, folk, and traditional blues music, and it was first developed by Black Americans in the 1940s.

Success and Sadness

The second Destiny's Child album, *The Writing's on the Wall*, came out in July 1999. It was a much more personal album than the group's first one, because Beyoncé cowrote and coproduced many of the tracks. Since Beyoncé had more creative control on this project, she made sure that the songs involved themes that were important to her, like female empowerment.

The album's lead single, "Bills, Bills, Bills," became the group's first song to hit number one on the *Billboard* Top 100. But even though Destiny's Child was soaring higher and higher, there was turmoil within the group. Two of the girls, LeToya and LaTavia, felt they weren't being given the spotlight as often as Beyoncé and Kelly, whether they were recording songs or dancing onstage. Was it true? Depends on who you ask. Beyoncé was normally the group's peacemaker, but in this case, there was a rift she couldn't mend. And it really upset her.

"Bills, Bills, Bills" is about a woman whose significant other takes things from her without paying her back.

For instance, he maxes out her credit cards and drains her car's gas tank.

Thriving and Surviving

By January 2000, LeToya and LaTavia had left Destiny's Child. Shortly afterward, two new members joined the group: Tenitra Michelle Williams (often simply known as "Michelle") and Farrah Franklin. And while Farrah was only there for a few months before leaving, Michelle soon became an integral part of the group.

Sometimes, reporters and radio show hosts would mock Beyoncé by discussing who was leaving the group next. One radio deejay jokingly compared Destiny's Child to the reality show *Survivor*, where a different contestant is voted off each week. Beyoncé, sick of all the taunting, cowrote a song called "Survivor," about persevering and staying strong despite what life throws at you. *Survivor* was also the title of Destiny's Child's third album, which was released on May 1, 2001.

The album debuted at number one on the *Billboard* chart. Indeed, Beyoncé was proving that despite the jeers and mockery, she was in fact a survivor.

BEY BITS!

One of the songs on *Survivor*, "Independent Women Pt. I," was Destiny's Child's third number one single, after "Bills, Bills, Bills" and "Say My Name."

But before it appeared on *Survivor*, "Independent Women Pt. I" first appeared on the soundtrack to the 2000 Drew Barrymore film *Charlie's Angels*.

Fierce Facts

1. The first Destiny's Child song the general public heard was "Killing Time," which was released on the soundtrack album for the Will Smith sci-fi classic *Men in Black* in June 1997.

2. "Say My Name" is about a woman who's on the phone with her boyfriend, but he refuses to say her name during the phone call, and she suspects he's cheating on her.

3. Beyoncé cowrote the song.

4. In 2001, "Say My Name" won a Grammy Award for Best R&B Song.

5. It also won the Grammy for Best R&B Performance by a Duo or Group with Vocals.

6 Those were the first two Grammys that Destiny's Child ever won.

7 "Independent Women Pt. I" spent eleven weeks at the number one spot on the *Billboard* Hot 100 chart.

8 "Independent Women Pt. I" was a tribute to independent women everywhere who work hard and are self-sufficient.

9 On May 8, 2001, a week after *Survivor* debuted, Beyoncé starred in the made-for-TV movie *Carmen: A Hip Hopera*.

10 The film was a hip-hop reimagining of French composer Georges Bizet's 1875 opera *Carmen* with Beyoncé as the main character, Carmen Brown.

Museum Musings

"My mother is a huge art collector and she always encouraged me from a young age to invest in art. I travel a lot and I love going to art galleries and museums in different cities with my family and friends."

—Beyoncé on her love of art

Have you ever been to an art gallery or a museum? What was it like? What kind of art do you like looking at? Paintings? Sculptures? Something else? Write about it on the lines below.

_____
_____
_____
_____
_____
_____
_____
_____
_____
_____
_____
_____
_____
_____
_____
_____
_____
_____
_____

Your Secret Self

Beyoncé has said that when she was a teenager, she was so shy and quiet, her classmates didn't know that she could sing. That's because she hardly spoke when she was around them. What is something that the other kids at school don't know about you? Do you have a hobby, talent, or area of interest they don't know about? Write about it on the lines below.

_____
_____
_____
_____
_____
_____
_____
_____
_____
_____
_____
_____
_____
_____
_____
_____
_____
_____

Queen Bey Quiz: Teamwork Makes the Dream Work

1) Before Girl's Tyme became Destiny's Child, the group was briefly known as ____.

   a. Chip 'n Dale's Rescue Rangers
   b. Duck Tales
   c. Something Fresh
   d. Goof Troop

2) Beyoncé would sometimes get ideas for songs from listening to the customers in her mom's ____.

   a. Space station
   b. Medieval castle
   c. Superhero headquarters
   d. Hair salon

3) In 1999, Destiny's Child performed as the opening act for which R&B group?

   a. The Barden Bellas
   b. TLC
   c. Daisy Jones and the Six
   d. The Partridge Family

4) Before pursuing a career in music, Michelle Williams studied ____ in college.

    a. Levitation
    b. Pulling a rabbit out of a hat
    c. Criminal justice
    d. Card tricks

5) *Carmen: A Hip Hopera* first aired on ____.

    a. MTV
    b. The Archery Channel
    c. The Ballpoint Pen Channel
    d. The Silverware Channel

Check your answers on page 78!

GOING SOLO

Dangerously Daring

In 2001 and 2002, Beyoncé, Kelly, and Michelle went on tour to promote *Survivor*. But after the tour ended, Destiny's Child decided to take a break for a while so that each of the women in the group could concentrate on solo projects.

Beyoncé's solo debut, *Dangerously in Love*, was released on June 23, 2003. Before the album came out, some thought that Beyoncé lacked the star power for a successful solo effort. But it was a massive success, debuting atop the *Billboard* 200 chart. The album's first single, "Crazy in Love," held the number one spot on the *Billboard* charts for eight weeks. Beyoncé proved the naysayers wrong.

Dangerously in Love was Beyoncé's meditation on the various stages of love.

The album sold eleven million copies worldwide!

Happy B'Day

By 2004, Destiny's Child resumed working as a group. And on November 15 of that year, their fourth album, *Destiny Fulfilled*, was released. Beyoncé, Kelly, and Michelle toured to promote the album. But by the time they went onstage for the last stop of the tour, in Vancouver, Canada, on September 10, 2005, they decided that their time together as Destiny's Child was over. The three women announced that the group would be splitting up. They would remain close friends. But they would no longer perform together.

Once the tour ended, Beyoncé began developing her second solo project. She wanted to create an album that would speak to *all* women. Beyoncé cowrote many of the album's songs, and her songwriting partners included her sister Solange and her cousin Angie. The result was *B'Day*, which was released internationally on September 4, 2006. The album's title had a special meaning, because it came out on Beyoncé's twenty-fifth birthday.

Whereas *Dangerously in Love* was largely about the joys of romance, in *B'Day*, Beyoncé wanted to channel the emotions felt by a woman who'd just been dumped by her boyfriend.

While *B'Day* was issued worldwide on September 4, 2006, it was released in the United States on the following day (September 5).

Call Her Sasha!

Way back when Beyoncé was a seven-year-old performing in that first-ever talent show, she overcame her shyness by coming up with an alter ego: a brash, uninhibited, confident persona she would portray when onstage. Ever since then, whenever Beyoncé had to perform in front of an audience, she would transform into this stage persona. At first, the alter ego didn't have a name, but eventually, Beyoncé called her "Sasha Fierce."

And on November 12, 2008, Beyoncé officially introduced Sasha to the world when she released the two-disc album *I Am ... Sasha Fierce*. The first disc, "I Am," featured slower, softer, more heartfelt songs like "Halo." The second disc, "Sasha Fierce," was jam-packed with louder, faster, rap- and dance-inspired numbers like "Single Ladies."

The song "Single Ladies" became a huge hit, and it boasted over four million digital downloads.

On April 4, 2008, Beyoncé married rapper Jay-Z (aka Shawn Carter), after dating him for six years.

Not Just a Number

After the release of *I Am... Sasha Fierce*, Beyoncé went on a bit of a personal journey. In 2010, she took some time off from making music while she relaxed and traveled the world. By the time she resumed working in 2011, she had formed her own company, Parkwood Entertainment, which would produce some of her albums and movies. And she decided that her father, Mathew, would no longer be her manager. Beyoncé still loved her dad, but she wanted to be in charge of *every* facet of her brand.

All of these things made Beyoncé look at life differently, and as a result, her next album was a slight departure from what came before it. The album, *4*, which came out on June 24, 2011, was simpler, more mature, and more streamlined than the glossy and flamboyant *I Am... Sasha Fierce*.

BEY BITS!

One of the biggest hits on 4 was "Run the World (Girls)," which—like "Single Ladies" and "Independent Women Pt. I"—was an ode to female strength and empowerment.

"Run the World (Girls)" was also a fusion of electropop and R&B, which was a new sound for Beyoncé at the time.

Fierce Facts

1 In total, *Dangerously in Love* was nominated for six Grammy Awards.

2 The theme of *Destiny Fulfilled* was friendship.

3 Beyoncé cowrote and coproduced all the songs on *B'Day*.

4 On December 15, 2006, a film called *Dreamgirls*—starring Beyoncé—opened for limited release in theaters.

5 The movie was based on the Broadway musical of the same name.

6 Deena Jones, the character Beyoncé played in *Dreamgirls*, was loosely based on the legendary singer Diana Ross.

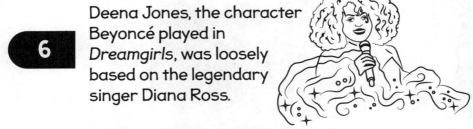

7 When Beyoncé was young, she was a fan of Diana Ross's music.

8 The full title of "Single Ladies" is "Single Ladies (Put a Ring on It)."

9 Some of the songs on *4* are tributes to artists who influenced Beyoncé.

10 For instance, "Love On Top" is a salute to Whitney Houston, Stevie Wonder, and other great singers Beyoncé grew up listening to.

Finding Focus

"Over time, I have learned to focus on the things I want to focus on in the time frame that I set. I no longer have to work based on someone else's expectations or pressure."

—Beyoncé on focusing

Do you find that you're able to do things in a better way when you focus on one thing at a time? Why do you think that is? Can you think of any examples of moments when you felt particularly focused? Write about it on the lines below.

Your Favorite Number

Beyoncé's favorite number is 4. That's why her fourth album is called 4. (Well, that and the fact that it's her fourth album.) She considers 4 to be her lucky number. After all, she was born on September 4, and her husband, Jay-Z, was born on December 4. And when Destiny's Child released their first album in 1998, there were four members in the group. Do you have a favorite number? What number is it? Is this number tied to a special occasion or something good that happened to you? Write about it on the lines below.

_____
_____
_____
_____
_____
_____
_____
_____
_____
_____
_____
_____
_____
_____

Queen Bey Quiz: On Her Own

1) *Dangerously in Love*'s first single, "Crazy in Love," featured Beyoncé teaming up with which well-known rapper?

    a. Oscar the Grouch
    b. Big Bird
    c. Jay-Z
    d. Abby Cadabby

2) After their 2005 announcement that Destiny's Child was disbanding, Beyoncé, Kelly, and Michelle briefly reunited the following year for an official farewell performance, singing the ____ right before the 2006 NBA All-Star Game.

    a. *Paw Patrol* theme song
    b. National anthem
    c. *SpongeBob SquarePants* theme song
    d. *Rugrats* theme song

3) The music video for "Single Ladies" was so popular, it inspired a ____.

    a. Breakfast cereal
    b. Breakfast burrito
    c. Breakfast sandwich
    d. Dance craze

4) Beyoncé's fans call themselves ____.

   a. The BeyHive
   b. Swifties
   c. The BTS ARMY
   d. Selenators

5) In 2006, Beyoncé played a character in the film *The Pink Panther*. Which character did she play?

   a. The Pink Panther's agent
   b. The Pink Panther's accountant
   c. Xania
   d. The Pink Panther's lawyer

Check your answers on page 78!

Part IV

DIFFERENT THEMES, DIFFERENT GENRES
Beyoncé (The Album)

On December 13, 2013, Beyoncé did something nobody thought possible: She released a surprise album, which was called *Beyoncé*. Only a few people had known of its existence. There was no advance publicity, no advertisement. Somehow, one of the most famous people in the world had managed to keep the album's existence a complete secret until its launch date without anyone catching on, which was quite a feat.

The album was a celebration of how Beyoncé felt: as a Black woman, as an artist, and as a new mom. But if there was no prior publicity for *Beyoncé*, would people know to buy the album? Would it be a success?

It sold a million copies all over the world in six days.

Beyoncé's self-titled album was her fifth album to hit number one on the *Billboard* charts.

It was also her fifth album, period.

When Life Gives You Lemons...

On April 23, 2016, Beyoncé released *Lemonade*, a bold and brilliant album in which many of the songs dealt with themes of female identity and Black agency. For instance, in the song "Formation"—and in its accompanying music video—Beyoncé tackled issues like beauty standards for Black women and police brutality.

Beyoncé also explored other topics—like rocky relationships—on *Lemonade*. By being brave and using her music to examine serious issues, Beyoncé created a truly unique album. It was nominated for nine Grammy Awards and ended up as the best-selling album of 2016.

BEY BITS!

Beginning with the release of the "Formation" single in February 2016, Beyoncé has shown her support for the Black Lives Matter movement, a group of activists advocating for the rights and fair treatment of Black people.

Hattie White was Jay-Z's grandmother. The title of Beyoncé's album *Lemonade* was inspired by something Hattie had once said: "I was served lemons, but I made lemonade."

Renaissance Woman

In the early 2020s, during the COVID-19 pandemic, Beyoncé found an escape from stress by making music and focusing on joy. The result was the 2022 album *Renaissance*, a less heavy effort than *Lemonade*. But even though Beyoncé wasn't dealing with weighty social and political topics this time around, she still gave her all in making this album.

Many of the songs on *Renaissance* serve as a celebration of the history and evolution of dance music, house music, and club culture. For instance, the closing track, "Summer Renaissance," is an homage to disco superstar Donna Summer.

BEY BITS!

Renaissance wasn't the *only* project Beyoncé had worked on between 2016 and 2022.

In 2018, she teamed up with her husband, Jay-Z, to record the album *Everything Is Love*. And in 2019, she released *The Lion King: The Gift*, a companion album to the *Lion King* movie remake that came out the same year.

The Roots of Country

When Beyoncé was a child in Houston, Texas, that city's cowboy culture made quite an impression on her, as did country music. And one of the tracks on *Lemonade*, "Daddy Lessons," is a country song. But on March 29, 2024, she released an album full of country songs, titled *Cowboy Carter*. And just as *Renaissance* explored the role Black communities played in the creation of house music, *Cowboy Carter* explored the role Black artists played in the creation of country music.

The first single from *Cowboy Carter*, "Texas Hold 'Em," became an instant hit when it was released on February 11, 2024. It quickly rose to number one on the *Billboard* Hot Country Songs chart, making Beyoncé the first Black woman to have ever topped that particular chart. Then it shot to number one on the *Billboard* Hot 100.

Country music isn't the *only* genre represented in *Cowboy Carter*.

There are folk, gospel, hip-hop, and pop songs on the album as well.

Fierce Facts

1 One of the songs on *Beyoncé*, which was called "***Flawless," included a sample of Nigerian author Chimamanda Ngozi Adichie's TED Talk "We Should All Be Feminists."

2 A visual album is a type of album that is accompanied either by music videos for every song or by another cinematic counterpart of some sort (e.g., a full-length movie or longform video).

3 You might think of visual albums as a combination of music, video, and film.

4 Beyoncé has released a few visual albums over the years.

5 *B'Day*, *Beyoncé*, and *Lemonade* are all visual albums. They are albums that have corresponding cinematic counterparts.

6 And the cinematic counterpart to *The Lion King: The Gift* was the film *Black Is King*, which premiered on Disney+ in 2020.

7 Beyoncé not only created the album *The Lion King: The Gift*, she also played the role of Nala in the 2019 *Lion King* movie.

8 House music is a type of up-tempo electronic dance music that was originally created in the 1970s as a fusion of American disco music and Eurodisco.

9 It's a genre of music that was largely created by Black and Latinx artists, many of whom were also members of the LGBTQ+ community.

10 In April 2024, Beyoncé released a *remixed* version of "Texas Hold 'Em," which included new lyrics.

Setting Boundaries

"Throughout my career, I've been intentional about setting boundaries between my stage persona and my personal life."

—Beyoncé on setting boundaries

Setting boundaries means creating guidelines and rules for how you want to be treated and how you want to interact with others. Why do you think setting boundaries is so important? What happens if you *don't* set boundaries with the people in your life? Write about it on the lines below.

_____
_____
_____
_____
_____
_____
_____
_____
_____
_____
_____
_____
_____
_____
_____
_____
_____

Named After You

Beyoncé is so famous that there's even an insect named after her! In 2012, a researcher from the Commonwealth Scientific and Industrial Research Organization (CSIRO) in Australia dubbed a previously unnamed species of horsefly the *Scaptia (Plinthina) beyonceae*. If there was an animal named after you, which animal would it be? Would it be a mammal? Insect? Bird? Reptile? Write about it on the lines below.

_____
_____
_____
_____
_____
_____
_____
_____
_____
_____
_____
_____
_____
_____
_____
_____

Queen Bey Quiz: Complete the Lyric

As a Beyoncé fan, you know the words to every one of her songs, right? Let's see just how well you know them! Fill in the blanks below to complete these Beyoncé song lyrics:

1) "If you liked it then you should've put a ____ on it"

   a. ring
   b. mustache
   c. beard
   d. wig

2) "Nine times out of ten, I'm in my ____"

   a. swimming pool
   b. feelings
   c. shower
   d. jacuzzi

3) "Baby I can ____ your halo, you know you're my savin' grace"

   a. draw
   b. paint
   c. sculpt
   d. see

4) "You're the ____ that gives your all"

    a. vampire
    b. werewolf
    c. one
    d. mummy

5) "Some call it arrogant, I call it ____"

    a. confident
    b. sauerkraut
    c. tuna fish
    d. egg salad

Check your answers on page 78!

Part V

FILMMAKING AND FUTURE ENDEAVORS
Documentary Director

Beyoncé isn't just a consummate entertainer. She also knows how to really put on a show. Her concerts are famed for their spectacle. Ever the multitasker, Beyoncé decided to codirect a concert documentary about her world tour to promote *Renaissance*. That documentary, *Renaissance: A Film by Beyoncé*, was released on December 1, 2023.

A peek behind the curtain, the movie showed Beyoncé training, rehearsing, and performing. It was all there: the dazzling haute couture outfits! The elaborate sets! The backstage drama! In this film, Beyoncé wasn't afraid to show the viewer a glimpse at the moments when things went awry. In one scene, the sound cut out in the middle of a song, forcing Beyoncé to run offstage.

The critically acclaimed film is a gift for anyone who ever wanted to know how the magic was made.

Renaissance: A Film by Beyoncé isn't Beyoncé's first project as a director.

She has also directed—or in some cases, codirected—various music videos, long-form videos, and documentaries, including 2016's Lemonade (the hour-long video experience that accompanied the album) and the 2020 Disney+ film Black Is King.

Infinite Possibilities

During her career, Beyoncé has evolved from lead vocalist to solo artist, from pop star to multimedia mogul. And in all that time, she's gained more creative control over her music, and she's tackled serious issues in some of her projects. But her career's far from over. What will the future bring for Beyoncé?

This is hard to say. After all, she often does what her audience least expects, from releasing a surprise album to creating a remarkably intimate behind-the-scenes documentary about her world tour. But based on the body of work Beyoncé has created thus far, her future is one of infinite possibilities.

In 2013, Beyoncé founded a charitable organization called the BeyGOOD foundation.

BeyGOOD was created to support under-resourced and underserved communities and programs.

Fierce Facts

1 Beyoncé's zodiac sign is Virgo.

2 Throughout her career, she has referenced this in songs like "Gift from Virgo," "Signs," and "Virgo's Groove."

3 In 2020, Beyoncé told a reporter from *British Vogue* that she has two beehives at her house.

4 She went on to explain that she has roughly eighty thousand bees and that she makes hundreds of jars of honey each year.

5 In 2010, Beyoncé performed in the Hope for Haiti Now charity telethon, a benefit for earthquake relief.

6 And in 2017, after Hurricane Harvey ravaged the city of Houston, Beyoncé returned to her hometown to serve food to the people affected by the disaster.

7 She was accompanied by her mom, Tina, and her former Destiny's Child bandmate Michelle Williams, both of whom also gave food to those impacted by the hurricane.

8 In 2023, Beyoncé teamed up with former bandmate Kelly Rowland to create thirty-one permanent housing units for the unhoused population in Houston.

9 When putting together *Cowboy Carter*, Beyoncé enlisted the aid of several music industry titans, such as Stevie Wonder, Miley Cyrus, Nile Rodgers, and Post Malone, all of whom either sang or played musical instruments on one of the tracks.

10 Also, country music legends Dolly Parton, Linda Martell, and Willie Nelson provided interlude narration in between the songs on the album.

Helping Others

"In 2013, I started [the] BeyGOOD [foundation] to share the mentality that we could all do something to help others, something my parents instilled in me from a young age."

—Beyoncé on helping others

What are some ways *you* help others? Do you volunteer for any organizations"? Do you donate food and clothing to unhoused people? Write about it on the lines below.

Role Models

When Beyoncé was young, she had lots of role models. Many of them were people in the music industry whom she admired, like Diana Ross, Prince, and Whitney Houston. These days, Beyoncé herself is a role model to so many people! Who are *your* role models? What industry do they work in? Are they family members? Teachers? Mentors? Musicians? Actors? Athletes? Scientists? Activists? Authors? Write about your role models on the lines below.

_____
_____
_____
_____
_____
_____
_____
_____
_____
_____
_____
_____
_____
_____
_____
_____

ANSWER KEY

Pages 18-19:
1) d, 2) b, 3) c, 4) a, 5) d

Pages 34-35:
1) c, 2) d, 3) b, 4) c, 5) a

Pages 50-51:
1) c, 2) b, 3) d, 4) a, 5) c

Pages 66-67:
1) a, 2) b, 3) d, 4) c, 5) a

ABOUT THE AUTHOR

Many years ago, when Arie Kaplan was first starting out as a freelance writer, he wrote a cover story on Destiny's Child for *Teen Beat* magazine. So you might say it was his *destiny* to write this book! (Sorry.) In addition to being a former entertainment journalist, Arie wrote the six-volume ShockZone: Games and Gamers series of children's nonfiction books, which covered every aspect of the video game industry. And he wrote the award-winning nonfiction title *From Krakow to Krypton: Jews and Comic Books*, which was a finalist for the National Jewish Book Award.

Aside from his work as a nonfiction author, Arie has written numerous books and graphic novels for young readers, including *Jurassic Park Little Golden Book*, *Frankie and the Dragon*, *LEGO Star Wars: The Official Stormtrooper Training Manual*, *The New Kid from Planet Glorf*, *Batman: Harley at Bat!*, *Spider-Man Comictivity*, *Shadow Guy and Gamma Gal: Heroes Unite*, and *Speed Racer: Chronicles of the Racer*. In addition, Arie is a screenwriter for television, video games, and transmedia. Please check out his website: www.ariekaplan.com.